Conspiracy Theory 101

A Researcher's Starting Point

Ava Fails

Disclaimer
Dedication
Introduction
Chapter 1: Conspiracy 101
    JFK Assassination
    September 11, 2001
    Roswell and UFO's
Chapter 2: Some Harsh Facts
    MK Ultra
    Operation Northwoods
    COINTELPRO
    Tuskegee
    Human Experiments and Biological Weapons Testing
    Fluoride
Chapter 3: The Problem with Conspiracies
    Government Transparency
    Whistleblowers
    The Media
    The Players
Chapter 4: A Losing Game
Chapter 5: Is Everything a Conspiracy Theory?
Chapter 6: Going Deeper
    Population Control
    Agenda 21
    Georgia Guidestones
    Bilderberg
    Benghazi
    Monsanto
Chapter 7: Waking the Masses
Chapter 8: This is Where it Gets CRAZY
    Silent Weapons for Quiet Wars
    Brice Taylor a.k.a. Susan Ford
    Ted Gunderson
    The Moon Hoax

Chapter 9: Further Reading and Research
    YouTube
    Websites
    Some Favorite Threads from AboveTopSecret.com
    Books
    Software
    Suggested Search Topics
Appendix 1: Links in Order of Appearance
Appendix 2: Reference Materials
Afterword
My Personal Views on Conspiracy Theories
    The Beginning
    Enter the Illuminati
    The Elites, Secret Societies and Lucifer
    Politics
    My View on Conspiracies
    The Historic vs. Scientific View
    A Rough View of the Big Picture
    Biblical Warnings of Things to Come
Bibliography

Disclaimer

© **2014 Ava Catherine Marcella Fails** *All rights reserved.* No part of this book may be reproduced or transmitted in any form or by any means, electronic or mechanical, including photocopying, recording or by any information storage and retrieval system, without written permission from the author, except for brief quotations in a review.

The inclusion of web links and ideas presented in this content does not indicate endorsement by the author of people, websites, content, or ideas.

If you enjoy this book, please check out these titles I've written under a pen name:

Did you know that American history is peppered with cases of human experimentation? Could you in your wildest dreams imagine that it was happening through the mid-1970s? That is in most of our lifetimes!
I wish that I could tell you that it's a load of crap, but the fact is...it's true. Supported by dozens of declassified documents and publications, horrible human testing can be corroborated throughout our history. Conspiracy Fact: Human Experimentation in the United States introduces you to a number of appalling cases involving the most vulnerable members of society.
The book documents a handful of cases taking place between the 1840s and 1970s. That's right, for over a century, these atrocities were regularly happening. This is just the tip of the iceberg. Get it today.

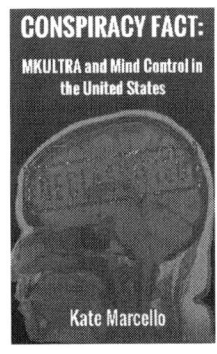

Mind Control in the United States?
Hard to believe? The series Conspiracy Fact Declassified is back again to prove it happened. Through declassified documents and various other sources, we further explore human experimentation. This time we zoom in specifically on mind control and the Top Secret government projects that examined this realm.
We name the names.
This compelling book is sourced throughout. You'll find out about how the U.S. ferried Nazi scientists into the country after World War II, and how that single operation became the catalyst for the creation of MULTIPLE experimental projects. You'll find out how those projects sourced more than 88 institutions nationwide to perform mind control experiments on unwitting citizens.
You will hear from survivors. Grab this one!

Visit my blog and sign up to my email list to be notified of future publications.

Dedication

I dedicate this book to God first.

Next, I dedicate it to my family, most of all, my dad who planted the seed. Love y'all.

For my friends. You contribute to my life daily and I love you all.

Finally, to all the researchers, Patriots, and truth-seekers. We might not all agree, but at the end of the day, we all want the same thing...TRUTH.

Introduction

I've been interested in conspiracy theories since I first heard my dad talking about the JFK assassination as a teenager. I've been an active member of various online conspiracy communities since 2008. I've read a TON of information and spent countless hours pouring over evidence trying to find viable conclusions to change the theory to fact. Instead, what has happened is I have found that truth is elusive. Not of its own accord, but it has been hidden, manipulated, and buried until even if you do find it, reasonable doubt still exists. I've found that the study of conspiracy theory is a conspiracy theory unto itself. As theorists, or as I prefer to be called "truth-seekers", we have created so much content, that we have further covered what we were looking for in the first place.

In this book, I will take you from Conspiracy 101 into some territory you may not have investigated before. I must warn you. The truth is hard to swallow. The truth is so shocking that you may find it unbelievable at times. In some cases, the truth is not the truth at all. I encourage you to do your own research, but more than this, I encourage you to keep your mind and emotions in check as you explore the evidence. The subjects presented here will change your worldview. They could easily alter your life and mental state in negative ways. I stress to you wholeheartedly that you only continue reading if your support and faith systems are strong. I don't say these things to scare you or present an alarmist front in any form. I say them to let you know this isn't light reading material.

Keep in mind that many of the subjects touched upon in this book have generated many books all by themselves. Much of the information provided in this book just touches upon the tip of the iceberg. There are researchers who spend their lifetimes on just ONE of the subjects I'll briefly cover here. **It is up to you to do your own research deeper into these subjects so that you might form your own educated opinion.** This is not easy knowledge to gain or accept. You cannot un-know these things.

NOTE: There are links provided throughout this book to various pieces of web content. All of these links will be provided again in the Chapter on Further Reading and Research for your convenience. I don't like to use Wikipedia as a source, but in some cases it is the only blanket source of general information on some topics. I have attempted in those cases to offer more specific sources for reference. In addition, the Chapter on Further Reading and Research will present information not mentioned or covered in this book. All of my previous cautions apply to this information as well.

Chapter 1: Conspiracy 101

I think more Americans believe there was a conspiracy that resulted in the death of our 35th President, than any other theory out there. The evidence, documentaries, and information for this one case is enough to keep one busy for years, but there's so much more. Here are a few of the most popular and controversial conspiracies out there in brief.

JFK Assassination

The general premise of the situation is that President John F. Kennedy rode through Dealey Plaza in Dallas, Texas on November 22, 1963. Shots rang out, and the resulting barrage of bullets ended with the President being fatally shot in the head. An event that was caught on tape by the famous film shot by Abraham Zapruder. [1]

The assassin, Lee Harvey Oswald, was caught the same day after shooting a Dallas police officer. Two days later, he was killed, again on camera, by Jack Ruby with one shot to the abdomen. The new President, former Vice President Lyndon Baines Johnson, put together the Warren Commission to investigate the assassination. They concluded that Lee Harvey Oswald acted alone, and closed the book on the case.

This conclusion meant that Lee Harvey Oswald, a former Marine with questionable marksman skills using an archaic bolt-action rifle, would have to fire 3 shots within 8 to 11 seconds. It required that he aim and fire at a moving target, pull back the bolt to release the shell, and then aim and fire again. He would aim and fire one more time before it was over, but was he the only one firing?

This wasn't good enough for the American people, and the case was revisited with a new investigation in 1978. The House Select Committee on Assassinations simply concluded that the killing was the result of a conspiracy, and that was it. For 50+ years, we have been left to theorize and hypothesize about what happened in Dealey Plaza that day.

A new idea was presented to the public on the 50th anniversary of the event in November 2013 that theorized the final shot that exploded Kennedy's head was accidental. This idea theorized that the shot came from a Secret Service agent in the follow-up vehicle. The agent had retrieved an assault rifle from the floorboard of the limo, and when the vehicle lunged, he fired the fatal shot. This action was followed by an extensive cover-up to save the agency from public embarrassment. I don't think we will ever know what really happened that day. [2]

September 11, 2001

There are not many people on this planet who don't know the significance of this date. The official story says that two planes flown by Middle Eastern terrorists slammed into the Twin Towers of the World Trade Center in Lower Manhattan. A little later, two more planes would crash...one into the Pentagon, and another into a field in Shanksville, Pennsylvania. More than 3,000 souls were lost that day including, first responders, plane passengers, and innocent people on the way to work or already there.

So, where's the conspiracy? Well, theorists say the whole thing was an inside job perpetrated by the U.S. government to launch the country into war because war is profitable apparently. There's a declassified document floating around out there that details Operation Northwoods. This was a Cold War era plan put together by the Joint Chiefs of Staff during Kennedy's term that outlined the supposed hijacking of commercial airliners which would then be replaced with drone duplicates and flown into targets in Cuba. The odd thing about this document is that it sounds a bit like exactly what happened on September 11, 2001.

That's not all. The plane crashes into the Twin Towers were caught by multiple cameras. By the time the second plane hit the South Tower, news crews were literally everywhere. The second hit is documented from multiple angles. Numerous discrepancies have been noted with the footage shot that day in addition to the events themselves.

Often unbeknownst to the public, another building also collapsed that day at the World Trade Center. Approximately 8 hours after the first impacts to the Twin Towers, World Trade Center Building 7 collapsed into its own footprint. Footage of the collapse looks very much like a controlled demolition. This building was not hit by an airplane, and didn't sustain significant damage from the collapse of the towers. September 11, 2001 was the first time in history that not one, but three, steel-reinforced buildings collapsed due to fire.

There were also other problems with the investigation like the lack of plane parts at all 4 scenes. Parts that were found and identified could have easily been planted. Odd things survived the plane crash, explosion, and building collapse like one of the hi-jacker's passports. In fact, there were so many problems that even 13+ years later, we are no further on sorting them all out. These problems were further complicated by the expedited manner in which the wreckage of the Towers was removed and disposed of even before the investigation was complete. At the Pentagon, the FBI confiscated 84 surveillance tapes from businesses surrounding the area. ONE loop that contained 5 frames of video was released to the media. This loop showed no plane hitting the Pentagon, it just showed the resulting explosion.

The Pentagon was hit on its western facade by a Boeing 757 jetliner. A 757 boasts a wingspan of nearly 125 feet. The tail height is 44 feet. To put it in perspective, that is 4 stories. The resulting "hole" in the Pentagon was found to be 75 feet wide by the ASCE Pentagon Building Performance

Report. This has caused numerous questions to result about what really hit the Pentagon. Theorists scream "conspiracy" because it seems this could be cleared up if they would release some of those tapes.

As for Shanksville, it is widely believed that the passengers aboard realized what was happening, and that this plane was most likely headed for the White House. As a result, it is believed the passengers overtook the hi-jackers resulting in the plane crashing into a random field. This crash didn't escape the scrutiny either. The crash in Shanksville failed to produce one piece of an airplane, one seat, or even one piece of luggage. This would be the first time in history that a plane completely vaporized on impact. The obvious questions have all been asked, but there are no obvious answers. [3]

Roswell and UFO's

In Roswell, New Mexico, something crashed on a farm in the summer of 1947. Newspapers broke the story, *RAAF Captures Flying Saucer on Ranch in Roswell Region*. By the next day, the flying saucer had turned into a weather balloon gone awry. However, the response for this weather balloon included a significant military presence, the removal of every scrap of evidence, and the exclusion of both media and citizens from the area. [7]

Thus began a swift succession of sighting after sighting of flying saucers and UFO's of all kinds...and more crashes. Each crash was handled with they same protocol. Media and citizens were not allowed in the area, and the military cleared the crash site of all debris. Eye witnesses sometimes claimed to see large flatbed trucks going into a site only to come out with whatever they were hauling amply covered. The sightings continued including one of a large UFO or UFO's over the Capitol building in 1952 which is still unexplained to this day. [8]

The UFO phenomena has remained over the years, and theories abound. Some think these craft hold space travelers from other solar systems. Some think it's just the military testing top secret aircraft. Whatever it is, the public is not being told, and it's not just happening in this country. Sightings, abductions, cattle mutilations, crop circles and other phenomena have happened and are happening world-wide. There are online resources, networks, associations, etc. that gather evidence and information to be shared among citizens, but the U.S. government remains silent.

In April of 2013, the Citizen Hearing on Disclosure met for a week and resulted in more than 30 hours of testimony and 40 witnesses to the UFO presence. This hearing was the largest gathering of its type including representatives from 10 countries. It is the most extensive body of evidence available to date concerning UFO's. [9]

These theories are here to stay. Man has theorized since the beginning of time. No fact has ever become a fact that wasn't a theory first.

Chapter 2: Some Harsh Facts

Some of the elements that make up the conspiracy community aren't theories at all. They have been corroborated through declassified documents, whistleblowers, or have simply been known to the public in a simpler form only to uncover the whole story at a later date. The following are a few examples.

MK Ultra

MK Ultra was the culmination of a few other government projects that evolved into Mind Kontrolle or control translated from German. Since the 1940's the government has tested various methods of mind control. This is indisputable fact based on declassified government documents. MK Ultra included things like drugs, namely LSD, sleep deprivation, and electric shock to make individuals compliant. The purpose for such experiments is unknown although the government would like us to think these methods were only researched for use on enemies in times of war.

The problem with MK Ultra is that, like the space program, we borrowed a good portion of our knowledge and research from former Nazis who were employed in the concentration camps during the second World War. Another problem with MK Ultra is that some test subjects were tested without their knowledge which resulted in damage both physically and mentally. Furthermore, many believe that MK Ultra is an ongoing project even though the government claims it fully ended in 1973. [10] President Clinton made a public apology for human testing in 1995.

Operation Northwoods

Operation Northwoods was the codename for a set of proposals regarding turmoil in Cuba in 1962. These proposals called for Intelligence operatives to basically fake terrorist attacks on various U.S. cities and other locations under the guise of the Cuban government in hopes of starting a war with them. Operation Northwoods was rejected by the Kennedy administration.

The goal was ultimately to create support among the American public for war with Cuba in the wake of these so-called terrorist attacks. Operations Northwoods was much more sinister than it sounds. The document which was declassified on November 18, 1997, included:

- A detailed attack on Guantanamo Bay
- Blowing up a U.S. ship in Guantanamo Bay, and blaming Cuba
- Developing a Communist Campaign in Miami and Washington
- Sinking a boatload of Cuban refugees on its way to the U.S.

- Threatening Cubans living in the U.S.
- Destroying U.S. military drone aircraft with F-86 planes painted to look like Cuban MIGs
- Staging attempted hijackings of civil air and surface craft
- Create an incident that convinces that a Cuban aircraft has attacked and shot down a U.S. chartered civilian airliner headed to Jamaica, Guatemala, Panama, or Venezuela from America
- Painting and numbering an aircraft to be an exact duplicate of of a commercial passenger jet. This duplicate would be substituted for the civilian plane, and loaded with passengers with aliases. The original plane would be converted to a drone. The 2 planes would be carefully coordinated with a rendezvous at Eglin Air Force Base. The drone will then send a MAYDAY signal from over Cuba reporting an attack by Cuban military aircraft.
- Using a small surface boat or submarine to disburse debris to fake a U.S. plane crash in Cuban waters. [11]

Yes, all of that is really contained in a document put together by the United States Department of Defense and the Joint Chiefs of Staff in 1962. This is fact. The government was willing to risk or even kill U.S. citizens to further its military and war agendas. Is it any wonder that there is distrust or that we question the validity of the "official stories" for events like 911? Are you awake yet?

COINTELPRO

COINTELPRO is short for the Counter Intelligence Program. It began the 1950's under then FBI Director, J. Edgar Hoover. It is essentially the precursor to the government spying and eavesdropping happening in more recent years. The Program targeted individuals and groups that were seen as radical such as the Ku Klux Klan, the Black Panthers, the Communist Party of America, and Dr. Martin Luther King, Jr. The Program sought to discredit such individuals involved in these groups and movements. [13]

Now, to some of us, it seems good that supposed hate groups like the Ku Klux Klan be discredited just like Al Qaeda or other groups that terrorize. However, it is now evident that in so doing, the freedom of innocent citizens is compromised. Tapping one phone seems to lead to tapping all the lines connected to that line, and it balloons from there until innocent and uninvolved citizens are being listened to for no reason. The Constitution provides the American people with protection from this as stated in the 4th Amendment:

> *"The right of the people to be secure in their persons, houses, papers, and effects, against unreasonable searches and seizures, shall not be violated, and no*

Warrants shall issue, but upon probable cause, supported by Oath or affirmation, and particularly describing the place to be searched, and the persons or things to be seized." [12]

The argument that if one has done nothing wrong, then they shouldn't be concerned is a travesty. If one has done nothing wrong, then they should retain their complete right to privacy.

The public wouldn't even be aware of COINTELPRO had a group of Vietnam War Activists not broken into an FBI satellite office in the early 70's and stolen documents that exposed the illegal methods the FBI was using against American citizens to gather information and enhance paranoia. [14]

Tuskegee

For 40 years, from 1932 to 1972, the United States Public Health Service ran a sinister study where 400 African-American men were intentionally infected with Syphilis. The men were treated with ineffective and sometimes harmful treatments while true treatment was withheld. The study was only supposed to last for 6 months, but it dragged on for 4 decades and nearly half of the unwitting participants died as a result. They also unknowingly infected their wives and fathered infected children. [15]

This happened. It happened in America. It happened in many of our lifetimes. The horrors and monstrosities were not always reserved for overseas dictators. Many of them happened right here carried out by your own government on citizens like yourself. Fact.

Human Experiments and Biological Weapons Testing

The United States has conducted some shocking test not only as human experimentation to learn about certain illnesses, but as biological weapons as well. Deeper than that, they have conducted this testing on American citizens as well as prisoners of war. This is scary, real fact. [16]

In 1941, working at the University of Michigan, Jonas Salk (he developed the polio vaccine) and other researchers deliberately infected patients at area mental institutions with Influenza to study the illness and treatments. [17] I don't think anyone would dispute the importance to eliminating illnesses such as Polio, but using human test subjects of low mental capacity or those who are unaware of the testing becomes a moral and ethical issue. It is simply wrong.

In the early 1940's, subjects at a Stateville Penitentiary in Joliet, Illinois were infected with Malaria to study the effects. Prisoners were offered various incentives to participate in the study that went on for 29 years. At least this time, the subjects were voluntary; however, something just feels wrong with using the prison population in this manner. [18] Not every prisoner is guilty of a horrible crime that would make such things seem somehow justified.

Between 1946 and 1948 in Guatemala, prostitutes were used in a study by U.S. researchers to infect prisoners, asylum patients, and soldiers with various sexually-transmitted diseases to study effective treatments. Approximately 700 people were infected including children conceived in the process. [19] Guatemala was chosen for this testing because it never would have flown in the United States. In 2010, when this experimentation was brought to light, the U.S. issued an official apology to Guatemala.

In 1950, the U.S. Navy used airplanes to spray San Francisco with an agent that was thought harmless at the time in order to simulate a biological warfare attack. Countless citizens contracted pneumonia-like symptoms and at least one person is reported to have died as a result. [20] These ridiculous simulations continued through 1969.

These experiments continued and included injecting people with live Cancer cells, spraying subway systems with agents, and infecting patients at mental hospitals with illnesses like Hepatitis. The moral and ethical issues with this type of experimentation are poignant, and the audacity of the U.S. Government to inflict such on citizens is appalling. While the need for experimentation to further Science is not in question, the ethical issues are questionable at best. How do we decide which citizens deserve the anguish of such experiments? "For the greater good" is neither an ethical justification, nor one that one would want to witness firsthand. "First, do no harm". [44]

Fluoride

Fluoride is good, right? This is how we keep our teeth strong and healthy. Fluoride was first added to drinking water in the United States in the 1940's to prevent tooth decay. However, if you have read the back of your tube of toothpaste, you know that it advises you contact Poison Control if more than a pea-sized amount is swallowed. Hmmm. So is it good or bad?

In 2011, the U.S. Government recommended changing the fluoride levels in drinking water for the first time in 50 years. This action was to reduce Fluorosis in children – a condition causing spotting and streaking of the teeth. Fluoride also has some unsavory side effects:

- Kidney and liver damage
- Calcification of the Pineal Gland
- Low Immune Function
- Infertility
- Lowered IQ

The days of water fluoridation should be in the past with greater access to fluoride products like toothpaste, mouthwashes, etc. Even so, fluoride could probably be removed from your daily hygiene without any negative result at all. Fluoride isn't so great. [21]

Chapter 3: The Problem with Conspiracies

There are a number of problems with conspiracy theories as a whole. The most significant being that conspiracy theories and those who entertain them are not socially accepted. Conspiracy theorists are somewhat of a fringe group that is not viewed positively by the government, the media, or society. Theorists who spill over into activism such as the 911 Truth movement or the Fukushima nuclear alarmists find the public a difficult audience for their ideas. It really drives home the fact that much of the information surrounding conspiracy theories are a heavy subject matter. It's a lot easier to hear about Justin Bieber getting arrested or what celebrity wore what at which award show. Anyone who is passionate about something knows that people can seem and most likely are apathetic to your cause. Let's look at some other issues.

Government Transparency

I don't have to tell you that there is no government transparency. Apparently, the American people are horribly ill-equipped to handle bad news. A good portion of the original JFK documents are still sealed. I believe the last batch is due to FINALLY be released in 2017. They are having hearings to decide if we are ready to hear about UFO's. We are spoon-fed the evidence to see how we will react. Mass hysteria must be avoided at all costs. We've never really been able to react to anything. We have been shielded from war on our own soil. For every tragedy or life obstacle, there is an equal and slow-to-react government program. We are kept in the dark under the guise of national security. In fact, national security is slowly robbing us of our rights and freedoms.

This isn't to say that government officials don't talk. They do. However, the government uses a method called compartmentalization. No one official ever has access to all facets of an operation. Instead, there will be several officials overseeing different aspects of the operation, and they will only be informed of, receive reports on, and have knowledge about one small part. The other parts would be handled by other teams of officials and at no time would the entire group as a whole meet together to discuss the operation in its entirety. Such discussions are reserved for a few select higher-ups.

Whistleblowers

These individuals are few and far between. A whistleblower is defined as: "one who reveals wrongdoing within an organization to the public or to those in positions of authority." [22]

Chelsea Manning formerly Bradley Manning

Chelsea Manning was a Private First Class in the Army when she was convicted in July 2013 on multiple charges including violating the Espionage Act, stealing government property, violation of the Computer Fraud and Abuse Act, and disobeying orders. She leaked an enormous cache of classified information including videos, 250,000 U.S. diplomatic cables, and 500,000 Army report known as the Iraq and Afghan War Logs. Most of the information was published on Wikileaks.org. She is currently serving a 35-year prison sentence as a result. [23]

Edward Snowden

Edward Snowden blew the top on the NSA when he released information on their spying practices which encompasses a massive surveillance of pretty much everyone. On June 5, 2013, Snowden began revealing Internet surveillance programs and the interception of U.S. and European telephone metadata. Snowden fled to Moscow via Hong Kong when the United States revoked his passport. On August 1, Russia granted him a one-year temporary asylum. Snowden said, his motive for releasing the information was, "to inform the public as to that which is done in their name and that which is done against them." Snowden is still in Russia as of this writing, and his next move is unknown at this time. He has charges pending should he return to the United States. [24]

These two examples are the most recent and high profile cases concerning people who released classified government information to reveal what they felt were wrongdoings to the American people. Whistleblowers release information at great personal risk. Chelsea Manning faced a possible death penalty if prosecutors pursued the "aiding the enemy" charge. They did not.

A couple of the videos that Manning released were telling about the American presence in Afghanistan. One video showed footage of an American helicopter attack on a journalist and two Reuters employees. A man in a van stopped to help the victims with his two young children in the vehicle. He was killed, and the children were wounded. The video was named *Collateral Murder* and released by Wikileaks.

The public and government reaction to whistle blowers are a mixed bag that falls somewhere between "hero" and "traitor".

The Media

People look to the media to get their facts. I hope I don't have to tell you the terrible fallacy in that. We watch the evening news to get the headlines of the day. If we change the channel, do the stories change from news agency to news agency? Not much. You might get a different view of a subject based on the political alignment of certain stations, but the headlines are usually the same. If it's Breaking News, you can almost bet you'll see the same crap on every news station.

You bet there's a conspiracy about the media too. At it's most basic, it's that the media is controlled by the government. The government tells the media what to report on, how to report it, and what not to say.

The Players
The Illuminati and Freemasonry

Illuminati means 'the enlightened ones". The Illuminati was started by a fellow named Adam Weishaupt on May 1, 1776. The group spread rapidly throughout Europe until motives to overthrow European monarchies was uncovered. The group's membership fell, and it was banned in Bavaria. [25]

It is widely believed that the Illuminati is closely related to Freemasonry, another secret society with questionable motives. Both groups present a Christian front to the public while it is believed that high-ranking members are aware of its Luciferian goals. Both groups also claim origins from the Knights Templar, yet another secret society.

Whatever the case, as John F. Kennedy said, "the very word secrecy is repugnant in a free and open society". [45] Secret Societies alienate people. It's disrespectful to emphasize one's social status by participating in a secret club of sorts. What is the point? The true intent is obviously of such importance that the lunacy of it all is necessary. It is commonly thought that the United States were founded on Christian principles when in fact, George Washington was an active Freemason and depictions of him laying the cornerstone for the U.S. Capitol building show him in full Masonic regalia. [12]

The New World Order

All the conspiracies, the corruption, all the secrets are wrapped up in a nice little package called the New World Order They've got the money to do it, control it, say who gets to know about it, and they have the money and power to cover it up so that you and I never find out about it. And if that's not enough, if we do find out, they will make us out to be crazy to the public. It happens everyday. You've probably heard it happen recently.

Odds are if you're going through the trouble to make an elaborate plan for world domination, you execute it, you keep people in the dark about it, and you've been successful so far, then you're going to have a back-up plan should any part of it fail. With money and power, all things are possible.

Chapter 4: A Losing Game

Unfortunately, all these powerful people seem to be psychopaths as well. They don't seem to care about you, your family, or anyone who is not a paid-off puppet furthering their agenda. If they do control everything, including the media, then they have the tools to classify anyone who gets in their way as a nut. Mainly, conspiracy theorists. Anyone who has the gumption to actually speak up and point an accusing finger is quickly given a free ticket on the crazy train. If that doesn't do a thorough enough job, then they release the disinformation hounds. Joe Schmo might have been barking up the right tree, but they will throw a wrench in that machinery by releasing a whole new theory. Now all the theorists are investigating and drooling over this other scenario because it's all new and shiny. It might even be better than the first idea; more plausible. Now the first theory and theorist are discredited by this new idea, and BOTH theories are discredited by the other. When you have a theory, you need evidence that to corroborate your first idea, not obliterate it.

Pretty soon, there are multiple theories surrounding one event. Each side has a staunch following in the conspiracy community, but what you don't have is an answer. You have all this content that has been generated about all the many aspects, and nothing solid. Any attempt to simplify this situation means taking backward steps in the process. It's like trying to untangle the Christmas lights only there are 1,000 strands of hundreds of multi-colored lights, and you only have 5 minutes.

What kind of "powers" would these "powers" be if they didn't have Plan A, Plan B, and a bonus backup plan. Even if you can prove a theory beyond reasonable doubt, even if you could untangle the Christmas lights, the sleepers like sleeping. No one wants to hear what you have to say because it will upset their lives in an irrevocable way. Once you realize that corruption is rampant, and that it is more sinister than you could have possibly imagined, there is no going back. You have passed the point of no return.

If indeed, any of this true, the world...America will never be the same, and it will never be what we thought it was when we bought into the dream of a spouse, two kids, a dog, a house, and white picket fence. No one wants to accept that they are a slave. No one wants to believe the things they have worked for their entire lives are all a worthless facade. Doom and gloom, people call it. It's the reality one accepts to be a conspiracy theorist. It's easier to stay asleep. It's a lot easier.

Chapter 5: Is Everything a Conspiracy Theory?

If you've ever read the posts on a conspiracy forum or blog, then you know the simple answer is "yes". Let's entertain a scenario. Let's say the government has just revealed the moon landing was indeed a hoax. It was all shot on a movie sound stage. They disclose the reason for this fakery was to maintain America's status as a superpower. They even present some good points about the fragility of the foreign political climate so soon after WWII, etc. You almost sympathize with them.

Now, how do we know what's the truth, and what's a lie? If we didn't land on the moon, then did we really find the Titanic in 1985? Was Lee Harvey Oswald really a lone, crazed gunman? Does Area 51 exist? Was that really a weather balloon in Roswell? There would be no end to the questions, and there would be no trust in the answers.

It's the same now. The silence is just as bad as admitting the lies. It's only natural. If a child eats a cookie without permission and you ask them if they ate the cookie, what would you think if they responded with just silence. If they didn't eat the cookie, they will either answer "no" or construct an obvious lie. Conspiracy theories are a response to obvious lies...and silence.

So, the not-so-simple answer is, yes, too. Everything is a conspiracy. Every "official story" is approached with a skeptical eye. Then the "official story" is put head to head with the evidence however limited it might be. The holes in the story are filled with theories, and boom, conspiracy!

Seriously. Research some current or recent events. All you have to do is put the words "hoax" or "false flag" after the headline and I am almost positive you will find a conspiracy theory relating to the event. That skeptical eye is much to the detriment of the conspiracy theorist. When you look at an event like the shooting at Sandy Hook Elementary in Newtown, Connecticut, the general public views the accusations made by conspiracy community as disrespectful and the allegations ludicrous.

Chapter 6: Going Deeper

So, how are you doing with this information so far? Are you managing to take it all in without hating the messenger (me)? Is your skepticism hardening you against the thoughts? Are you on board, but holding your own against the negative feelings one might experience? Are you falling apart? Does your life seem like a dismal and meaningless happening on a this doomed third rock from the sun? If you are experiencing any or all of those last few, take a break. Stop reading for a couple days and give your mind and heart time to process what you have learned so far. **I promise you, there is hope.**

If you're still with me, we are going a little deeper. Brace yourself for the next level.

Population Control

As of this writing, the world population has topped 7 billion people. Governments attempt to control population usually through mandates that limit the birth rate as can be seen in China with their one child policy. Some additional methods to control population include:

- Contraception
- Abstinence
- Medical Abortion
- Emigration

- Decreasing Immigration
- Sterilization
- Euthanasia

If you are unfamiliar with any of these terms such as Euthanasia, you might be surprised to find that it is defined as: *the act or practice of killing or permitting the death of hopelessly sick or injured individuals (as persons or domestic animals) in a relatively painless way for reasons of mercy.* [46]

We are sold the idea of population control under the guise that fewer people means a better standard of living for the rest of us. Sounds good, right? I could get on board with an easier, less-crowded commute to work. How about you? The problem resides in the methods used to reduce population,, the misleading terms being used to describe population control, and the people who are pushing this agenda.

Population control is being camouflaged behind terms such as "population stabilization", "immigration control", and other ambiguous terms. What it all boils down to is the theory that there is a "shadow government" that is utilizing many of the methods mentioned in this book such as chemtrails, fluoride, and vaccines to essentially reduce the population over time. It all fits neatly under the umbrella of Agenda 21 and the elements of a New World Order. [26]

The people who are advocating for population control and ultimately population reduction are an interesting bunch. Get a load of some of these quotes:

- *"If I were to be reincarnated, I would wish to be returned to Earth as a killer virus in order to contribute something to solve overpopulation."* - Prince Philip, 1988
- *"...if voluntary birth reduction methods did not work, a nation might have to resort to the addition of a temporary sterilant to staple food or the water supply."* *"Each person we add now disproportionately impacts on the environment and life-support systems of the planet."* - Dr. Paul Ehrlich, Science Advisor to George W. Bush
- *"The most merciful thing a large family does to one of its infant members is to kill it."* - Margaret Sanger, Founder of Planned Parenthood
- *"Right now there are just too many people on the planet. A total world population of 250-300 million people, a 95% reduction from present levels, would be ideal."* - Ted Turner, Owner of CNN, TNT, and others
- *"The world today has 6.8 billion people. That's heading up to about 9 billion. If we do a really great job on new vaccines, health care, reproductive health

services, we could lower that by perhaps 10 to 15 percent." - Bill Gates, Founder of Microsoft

It doesn't take much digging to find many, many more. Quotes are shaky ground because they can be so easily taken out of context. The importance of conducting more in-depth research cannot be stressed enough.

NOTE: These quotes are cited under one blanket website. [27] However, a Google search will result in multiple online and/or book sources.

Agenda 21

Agenda 21 was born in 1992 from the UN Conference on Environment and Development in Rio de Janeiro, Brazil. It is a 300-page document that touts a lot of information about combating poverty, changing living conditions, and promoting health amongst the population. [29] As with most documents of its kind, it is such an extensive body of writing that it's difficult to discern the indications of negative regulations in order to achieve the objective of the agenda itself. Many theorists believe that the ultimate goal of Agenda 21 is population control at best. [28]

Vaccines

It is a common idea that vaccines are being used to this end. Something is is supposed to protect the population from crippling illness could be the cause of just that, and in some cases, death. Vaccines have been linked on numerous occasions to Autism in the last 20 years. A fact that has been covered up and denied by sources such as the Center for Disease Control, and the National Geographic Society who released an article to the contrary. A court quietly confirmed in 2013 that the Measles, Mumps, Rubella vaccine can cause Autism. [30] To me, this is fact and it's personal. When my nephew received his 12-month shots, his development ceased and even digressed. He recovered, but it took the better part of 3-4 years.

A huge part of this is the Flu Shot and the controversy surrounding the 2010 H1N1 epidemic. The FDA scrambled to release enough vaccine to remedy the situation, and appropriate testing was pulled into question when people began having adverse reactions to the shots. Not to mention, that the Flu Shot doesn't always protect against the Flu and the ingredients are insane. [31]

Chemtrails

Chem what? Chemtrails are the cloudy tracks left behind by jet airplanes. More commonly known as contrails, chemtrails assert that many of these trails contain chemical by-products that are harmful. So, while contrails are accepted as a normal result of a jet engine in the low vapor pressure atmosphere, it is asserted that jets have been modified to spray chemicals to modify weather and/or shower the masses with what can essentially be called bio-weapons. Let's look at some evidence.

The most common form of weather modification is cloud seeding. Cloud seeding began as early as the 1940's and is used to make existing clouds produce precipitation. It has also been used to disperse fog banks near airports. This is fact and confirms that aircraft can be used to spray substances into the atmosphere.

In this video, a West Coast weather man explains some cloud bands visible on the radar as the "military dropping chaff" that contains bits of aluminum, plastic, and metalized paper products to throw off radar systems. He goes on to say that the military wouldn't confirm this, but he was the Marines for many years, and he is certain that is what's going on.

Chemtrails and weather modification fall under the umbrella of geoengineering which seeks to intervene and stop negative climate change by altering the Earth's natural systems. One method of doing this is the utilization of stratospheric aerosols to deflect sunlight. [32]

I don't know where this photo was taken. I have never seen a sky that looked like this even when I lived in Las Vegas, Nevada only minutes from McCarran International Airport. These grid patterns don't seem normal to me. Is this image the result of chemtrail spraying? I'm not sure, but I know that there are thousands of other images like this on the Internet. There is also video footage showing planes spraying. This footage depicts contrails that appear to turn on and off as the plane is flying. Is this solid evidence of nozzles spraying chemicals? You have to decide for yourself.

Eugenics

The word, Eugenics, comes from the Greek meaning "good/well". It's a study or social idea that by encouraging the reproduction of people with good genetic traits and discouraging the opposite, would advocate a more positive outcome in the evolution of the human race.

The modern concept of Eugenics was developed by Francis Galton in the 1860's and 1870's. Galton was the half-cousin of Charles Darwin and his work pulled many idea from Darwin's evolutionary writings and research.

Eugenics reached its height in the early 20th century. Policies and programs were put into place around the world by influential people and governments. These policies included, but were not limited to, genetic screening, birth control, marriage restrictions, segregation of races as well as the mentally ill from society, forced sterilization, forced abortions, forced pregnancies, and genocide. [33] It goes without saying that Adolf Hitler was a staunch proponent Eugenics.

The United States had jumped on the Eugenics bandwagon well before any programs became apparent in Germany. During the late 19th and early 20th centuries, Eugenics found wide support with the population because of racist issues and the desire to slow immigration from Europe. American Society during this time sought to strengthen the more dominant groups in the population. Eugenics gripped all areas of the country and was prominent in the academic community with universities offering hundreds of courses in the topic. [34]

Eugenics in the United States saw the formation of many agencies such as the Eugenics Record Office in New York and The American Breeders' Association. North Carolina had the most strict program of the 32 states with programs and it operated from 1933 to 1977. This particularly aggressive program allowed the sterilization of individuals with an IQ of 70 or below and social workers were endowed with the power to select individuals for sterilization based things like class and race. [35]

Eugenics went so far as to classify people based solely on their genetic contribution to society. People were classified as fit or unfit. Eugenics explored the idea of Euthanasia as well. Euthanasia was supposed to be the painless killing of those with incurable illnesses, old age, and whatever other reason could be concluded to terminate life. Eugenics is rarely talked about in the news, but I assure you it is alive and well today.

Georgia Guidestones

The Georgia Guidestones are a mysterious monument located in Elberton, Georgia, that has stood for more than 30 years. The stones address visitors as follows: *Let These Be Guidestones To An Age of Reason*. The stones display the following 10 declarations in 8 languages including Babylonian Cuneiform and Egyptian Hieroglyphics:

1. Maintain humanity under 500,000,000 in perpetual balance with nature
2. Guide reproduction wisely – improving fitness and diversity
3. Unite humanity with a living new language

4. Rule passion – faith – tradition – and all things with tempered reason
5. Protect people and nations with fair laws and just courts
6. Let all nations rule internally resolving external disputes in a world court
7. Avoid petty laws and useless officials
8. Balance personal rights with social duties
9. Price truth – beauty – love – seeking harmony with the infinite
10. Be not a cancer on the Earth – leave room for nature – leave room for nature

In addition, the stones also sport some complicated astronomical features. There is a slot cut in the center stone that frames the rising sun on the solstices and equinoxes. There is also a hole through which the North Star is located at all times. The capstone features a 7/8 inch aperture that aims a beam of sunlight to the corresponding date each day at Noon.

The stones are the brainchild of one man who goes by the pseudonym, R.C. Christian, and that's about all that is known about him. Wyatt Martin is a retired banker who helped broker the arrangement for the monument. R.C. Christian visited Elberton in 1979 and paid for the monument on behalf of a group of others living outside Georgia. Wyatt claims to have made an oath the mysterious R.C. Christian and he plans to take it to his grave. There are more details about their interaction in this article from *Wired* magazine.

Needless to say, in the silence and mystery of the man, R.C. Christian, conspiracy theories once again find a home. Seen as a monument to the New World Order, the stones have been vandalized on numerous occasions. The stones are now the property of the Elbert County and tended to by its officials. A time capsule is buried at the site as well, but an open date has never been specified. [36]

Bilderberg

The Bilderberg Group refers to an annual meeting of the world's elite. The first Bilderberg meeting was in 1954 at the Hotel De Bilderberg in Oosterbeek, Netherlands, hence the group name. David Estulin has been researching the Bilderberg Group for more than 14 years and has written a

book entitled *The True Story of the Bilderberg Group*. There are some intriguing truths about the Bilderberg Group:
- The membership is reserved for the world's power elite
- The meetings are never publicized and are accompanied by heavy security
- There is no apparent reason or result for the meeting

The proposed purpose has evolved to be that of a "shadow government" comprised of the best and brightest imaginable enacting policies that not brought before any government for debate or vote. The underlying purpose to design a One World Government also known as the New World Order. Because of the intense secrecy of the group, again these are only theories. Whatever the case, important and rich representatives from around the world meet for a weekend once a year to confer about something. [37]

Benghazi

Something happened in Benghazi, Libya on September 11, 2012. There's something about that date that I haven't quite unraveled yet. That night in 2012, an armed attack occurred on the American diplomatic mission killing U.S. Ambassador, J. Christopher Steven, among others. The attack consisted of 124 to 150 gunmen who sealed off the streets leading to the mission compound. While the compound included a safe haven, the Ambassador, another man, and a special agent aiding in the Ambassador's protection were overcome by smoke inside as the result of fires set by the attackers. In their flight from the safe haven, Ambassador Stevens was lost in the shuffle. Three phone calls went out to the Deputy Chief of Missions, Gregory Hicks in Tripoli. Hicks didn't answer because he didn't recognize the number...twice. Stevens managed to get through on the third call. A group arriving later from a CIA Annex a little over a mile away was unable to find Stevens. A Libyan militia group found his body in a smoke-filled room in the Ambassador residence. He was driven to the local medical center, but succumbed to asphyxiation from smoke inhalation.

    The attack was then surrounded in months of controversy as to whether it was a planned operation or street protest. When the former was emphasized, the U.S. government and more specifically, the Secretary of State, Hillary Clinton, was criticized for their lack of action. A response team assembled in Sicily, but was basically told to stand down because they would arrive too late, yet American lives were at stake. It was seen as a situation where the U.S. Government failed to do everything they could to save American lives in a hostile situation. [38] Hilary Clinton was removed as Secretary of State following the attack, and has since relayed that it was her biggest regret during her tenure. [39]

Monsanto

Few names wield a more sinister status than Monsanto. Most notable in recent news stories for their work in Genetically Modified Organisms (GMO's), Monsanto has been around since 1901. They are the company behind better known chemicals like Agent Orange and Round-Up (yes, the weed killer).

The evils of this company extend far and wide and they lord over a very important part of human life: the food supply. The problems with Monsanto:

- Their genetically modified seeds which contaminate the organic seed supply
- They manufacture seeds that are genetically engineered to produce their own pesticides
- Other countries have rejected the import of their GMO food products
- Their seeds produce plants that do not produce viable seeds
- They are attempting to monopolize the seed industry and have gone after small companies and farmers
- They put a great deal of money in lobbying for their own benefit

This is just a tiny portion of the problems with Monsanto and the extensive damage they are doing to the food supply, farming industry, and to humanity as a whole. [40]

Chapter 7: Waking the Masses

I think people are waking up now more than maybe ever. The Constitution equips the people with the power to overthrow corrupt government, but there are multiple problems with this. While the people are endowed with this option, there is no blueprint on how to even begin. The most noted movement in recent years that garnered a lot of attention was Occupy Wall Street.

Even though people are waking up, we are still an unorganized mass that is more apt to keep plans to themselves. More than that, we are easily distracted by the day to day. A large part of the reason we are drip-fed information is that we have the power as a people to overthrow anyone seeking to enslave us no matter how much money they have. There is no way for the government to truly know how many of us there are, or how much fire power we have at our disposal. They try to glean this information from things like the U.S. Census and gun permits and registration, but these things are inaccurate because not everyone participates.

If the information we have on the Illuminati is correct, then the U.S. government has been baby-stepping toward this end for more than 200 years. In recent years, the steps have grown larger and more frequent. Those in control are patient and long-suffering.

So, how might we approach people with information? Slowly, carefully, and sometimes not at all. A general approach is probably best. One that steers clear of religion and politics. These subjects tend to complicate things of this nature. If your personal approach to conspiracy theories is religious or political, and you are speaking with friends, then what is appropriate is at your discretion. In fact, conspiracy theories are a lot like religion and politics in that people will adamantly reject the content of your message if they don't want to hear it or they do not agree with it.

Not to mention you are up against individuals who have been programmed since birth to get their news, beliefs, and opinions from the media, music, and Hollywood. If they don't want to hear you, you cannot force them. It will have the opposite effect, and they will deem you a nut.

One way to open the door might be to bring up current events and find out their opinion. Ask them questions, give them your ideas, and go from there. Even if they stay asleep, you have planted a seed. They might go home and research what you've said only to find out more. You can bet they'll be back if that's the case. They might not, too, but that doesn't mean they won't remember what you said when an issue arises. They will think about it more thoroughly based on what you've said. Be careful who you trust.

Chapter 8: This is Where it Gets CRAZY

So, we've covered the basics of conspiracy theories and we have traveled a little deeper in, but we have managed to avoid anything too, too outlandish yet. Oh, you thought the idea that 911 being perpetrated by our own government *was* outlandish? Well, fasten your seatbelts, friends, because this is where it gets CRAZY.

Silent Weapons for Quiet Wars

Silent Weapons for Quiet Wars is the title of a document that William Cooper included in his 1991 book, *Behold A Pale Horse.* William Cooper was a conspiracy theorist and radio show host. He served in Navy, and used his service to make many claims about his Top Secret Q Clearance and access to classified information and documents.

The document is shocking to say the least. Cooper claims the document was found in an IBM copier that had been purchased at a surplus sale. The document opens by welcoming readers to the 25th anniversary of World War III. The document is dated May 1979.

Silent Weapons for Quiet Wars outlines much of the plan of the New World Order making numerous references to "the elite" and the "Bilderberg Group". Like many other theorists, William Cooper's legacy has two sides: those who believe him, and those who do not. [47] Cooper was killed by police in 2001 when they arrived on his property to serve him with an arrest warrant for threats. He shot at police first, and was taken down in the firefight. Those in support of him say his death was the result of mysterious circumstances and he was killed for releasing secret information.

Whatever the case, Cooper was somewhat of a pioneer of conspiracy theorists. He made some outlandish claims, but he spoke out with the absence of real fear. He woke a lot of people, and either way, it killed him in the end.

Brice Taylor a.k.a. Susan Ford

I'm reluctant to share the following book because it is so...I guess far-fetched is the best term I can use. This book centers around Mind Control, and if there is even a shadow of truth to any of it, we are and have been in serious trouble as humans. The evil of this age is bigger than anyone could imagine...if there is any truth here. The inclusion of this book is not my personal endorsement of the content because I have been unable to corroborate any facts in my research. Put on your Skeptic's Hat. You don't have to go far to find opposition to this story.

THANKS FOR THE MEMORIES
THE TRUTH HAS SET ME FREE !

The memoirs of
Bob Hope's and Henry Kissinger's
mind-controlled slave.
Used as a presidential sex toy and personal computer.

BRICE TAYLOR

Brice Taylor is an alias for a woman born Susan Lynne Eckhart Ford. In her book, Thanks for the Memories...The Truth Has Set Me Free! The Memoirs of Bob Hope's and Henry Kissinger's Mind-Controlled Slave, she recounts the trauma-based mind control she endured since birth with photographic detail. Her claims are unbelievable, yet this book has been out there for nearly 2 decades without opposition to her many accusations. "Unbelievable" is an understatement. She claims to have been used as a sex slave to several U.S. Presidents and as a sort of human hard drive for the likes of Henry Kissinger. She claims to have been sold by her father to Bob Hope at a sort of auction that masqueraded as a beauty pageant for children. The book is chock-full of detailed information about what Ford experienced until she was about 35 years old. She claims to have been deprogrammed after a decade of intense therapy. Here's a 10-minute video featuring Brice herself and in her own words.

This book is still for sale online as linked above for a rather steep price. Ford claims the revenue is being used to release her 3 children from mind control.

I found Susan Ford. She grew up in California and lived much of her adult life there, but it turns out that she is now residing in rural North Carolina. These days, she finds herself as an EEG tech. Here's the website featuring Brice/Susan right there on the home page:

http://www.eegcentreforneurofeedback.com/index.html

EEG Centre for Neurofeedback, LLC
In North Carolina since 1996
Susan L. Ford, CMC #1017 - Othmer Certified in Neurofeedback
828.475.6252

Home | About | What is Neurofeedback? | What is a qEEG? | Services | Insurance Questions | Testimonials | Links | Contact

Welcome to the EEG Centre For Neurofeedback

TRAIN YOUR BRAIN - CHANGE YOUR LIFE!
Neurofeedback, or EEG Biofeedback, is brain training. It is akin to exercising in the gym, only this training exercises your brain directly, with the objective of improving self-regulation. This in turn helps people function better, sleep better, and feel better. With improved self-regulation, individuals function well out of calm states, they are more even emotionally, and they are happier personally and in their relationships.

Neurofeedback is offered in a variety of health practices. I am neither a physician nor a psychologist. I offer this service on the basis of extensive specialized training and clinical practice for 17 years. Neurofeedback training is neither a medical treatment nor psychotherapy. The type of training I offer is not targeting any particular disorder or condition. It directly targets improved brain function. It is observed, however, that the symptoms of many disorders subside when this training is competently done.

Neurofeedback can teach your brain how to handle stress better, to handle challenges with greater ease, and to improve your performance in all walks of life. It works with children and adults alike and it's easy as your brain will be doing all of the work! No special effort is required on

One of our goals at the EEG Centre is to provide clients with information and resources for learning more about Neurofeedback.

As far as I know, as of this writing, this information is exclusive to this book. I guess the mind control memoir business wasn't lucrative enough?

Brice Taylor is not the only individual out there making these outlandish claims. Her story actually sounds a lot like that of Cathy O' Brien. There are also people who stand behind Brice and her claims like Ted Gunderson. I'll take a look at him in the next section. You're going to have to use your search skills if you want to explore further. If you pay attention to the below section of Video links, then you will have the opportunity to view testimony of other MKUltra survivors.

Ted Gunderson

Ted Gunderson was an FBI special agent. Ted worked on high-profile cases such as the death of Marilyn Monroe and the JFK Assassination. In his career, he worked out of numerous offices in major cities across the country. In the 1970's, he served as the head of the Memphis, Dallas, and Los Angeles FBI offices. [42]

After his retirement, he set up a private investigation firm in Santa Monica, California for a time. Gunderson warned about the New World Order. He made claims that a slave auction featuring children had been held in Las Vegas, 4,000 satanic ritual sacrifices occur in New York City on an annual basis, [41] he believed chemtrails were real, and he said the government had purchased 30,000 guillotines for use on citizens. [43]

Similar to William Cooper, Ted used his service to the United States to bolster his credibility. He supported Brice Taylor whole-heartedly.

The Moon Hoax

This is one of the more outlandish claims made by conspiracy theorists. It is theorized that man has never landed on the moon. That's right. We have dared to say that Apollo 11 and all subsequent moon missions were an elaborate lie. But why would the U.S. Government lie about that? To maintain superpower status, of course. In the 1960's, world powers, namely the United States and Soviet Union were in a maddening race to the Moon.

The Soviet Union was years ahead of America in the space race. They launched the first satellite, they sent up the first man into space, and the U.S. was clamoring for a piece of the action. After WWII, Operation Paperclip ensured that America secured the best and most brilliant Germany had to offer. Wernher Von Braun, along with more than 700 others were brought to the United States.[4] We wanted them all, and we got them even if it meant granting them immunity for WWII war crimes.

Whatever country made it to the moon first would certainly lay claim to any resources available there. In addition, if a country could get to the moon, then weaponizing space shouldn't be too far behind. The winner of the space race would be the most powerful country on planet Earth, and the United States must claim that title.

On July 20, 1969, we did when Apollo 11 landed on the Lunar surface and Neil Armstrong uttered the now famous words, "That's one small step for man; one giant leap for mankind." Or did we? The main points theorists like to bring up to say we didn't are:

- The Van Allen Radiation Belts. Every other space mission has remained well inside of these belts including the space station and space shuttles, but somehow we went through them in 1969.
- No crater under the Lunar lander. The Lunar lander was equipped with a rocket engine that delivered 10,000 pounds of thrust yet it left no crater on the Lunar surface which was soft enough to make perfect prints of the astronaut's boots.
- The flag planted by the astronauts appears to blow in the wind, but there is not atmosphere, air, or wind on the Moon.
- There are no stars depicted in the photographs taken on the Lunar surface.[5]

As with the Twin Towers, the footage from the moon has been evaluated and found to hold a number of inconsistencies...or does it? In 2011, NASA released new high resolution images of the Moon's surface showing various Apollo landing sites in detail. [6]

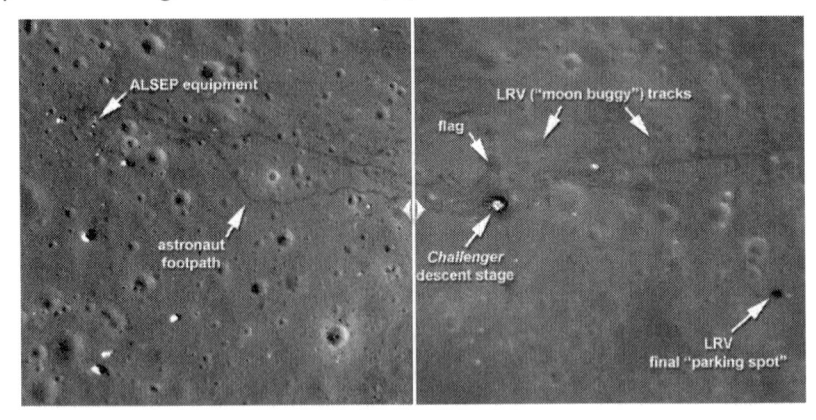

This is by no means even a fair sampling of some of the most outlandish theorists and theories out there. You've got your Big Foots, and Loch Ness Monsters, there's ghosts, aliens, chupacabras, mothmen, UFO landing sites, crop circles...it goes on and on. It's all a Google Search away or any good online forum will have categories dedicated to everything you've seen in this book.

Chapter 9: Further Reading and Research

As you continue your research, please keep in mind that it's not enough to find sources for information. You must also take into account who is behind the source. Who is doing the writing? Who is investigating? What are their motives? Should your research take you to a level of indisputable proof on any topic, you must source your information with reputable sources, and those reputable sources must be backed by reputable people.

The problem with this type of research is that everyone has a different idea as to who and what is a reputable source. For example, say you are using a clip from CNN to back a point about the 911 attacks. Some people will find this a reputable source since it's footage of the event as it happened. Others will say that CNN is a biased network and that Ted Turner is a paid-off government shill who only shows what the powers that be want him to show even if he has to fake it. There is opposition from every side, and honestly, I don't know how one might prove much of anything beyond a reasonable doubt these days.

Eventually, it comes down to is it proof enough for you? Are you willing to spread the word at the cost of fighting the opposition? Getting to the bottom of a theory is no small task. Personally, I research for myself. I research to be a well-informed citizen so that I can present an educated answer to common questions. I will tell you that "I don't know" is a common response for me.

YouTube

YouTube is a great source for information. There is a load of documentaries and informational videos on most any topic imaginable. I subscribe to a number of channels. Many of which have corresponding dedicated websites. Click around and explore.

Since YouTube is owned by Google, when you use Google Search, you will notice that the results return videos from YouTube at the top of the page. This is useful for obvious reasons, but also keep in mind that you can search directly from YouTube as well. I watch YouTube videos daily, and I usually just search and find something to watch after I check to see if any of my subscriptions have uploaded new videos.

NOTE: I will include the URL's to these channels and videos in the Appendix for those of you unable to click these links for any reason.

Channels

- [Stuff They Don't Want You to Know](#) – Short videos with lots of information
- [In The Know](#) – Lots of MK Ultra videos

- Dutchsinse – Lots of videos on weather modification and radiation
- The Political Port – Musings of one who is awake
- The Paulstal Service – Pointing out inconsistencies in the news
- All Time Conspiracies – Small chunks for the time-challenged; usually 3 minutes or less!
- Dark 5 – Just flat out interesting; not really conspiracies
- We Are Change – Non-profit, independent investigator, Luke Rudkowski
- David Von Pein's JFK Videos – All JFK, all the time. A lot of rare footage
- The Alex Jones Channel – A conspiracy profiteer in my humble opinion, but interesting content nonetheless
- Prophecy in the News – A lot of conspiracies discussed from a Biblical point of view

Videos

Some of these are pretty long. I'm only sharing videos that I found to be worth my time.

- Loose Change
- Leuren Moret Speaks on Fukushima
- The Fibonacci Sequence
- WACO: The Rules of Engagement
- The Men Who Killed Kennedy: The Coup D'etat
- The Men Who Killed Kennedy: The Forces of Darkness

- The Men Who Killed Kennedy: The Cover Up
- The Men Who Killed Kennedy: The Patsy
- The Men Who Killed Kennedy: The Witnesses
- The Men Who Killed Kennedy: The Truth Shall Set You Free
- The Men Who Killed Kennedy: The Smoking Gun
- The Men Who Killed Kennedy: The Love Affair
- The Men Who Killed Kennedy: The Guilty Men
- Agenda 21 The Depopulation Agenda
- MK Ultra Survivor Testimony
- What in the World Are They Spraying?
- A Funny Thing Happened on the Way to the Moon
- Sandy Hook Conspiracy
- Sandy Hook Case Closed
- Boston Bombing: What You Aren't Being Told
- Ruby Ridge
- Ruby Ridge Documentary
- UFO's, Aliens and Demons
- Demonic Alien Agenda
- Conspiritus
- Secrets in Plain Site
- I Almost Sold My Soul
- George Bush Sr. New World Order Clip
- George Bush Sr New World Order Speech from September 11, 1991   – There's that date again.

I could go on, but you must choose your own path of research. As you navigate YouTube and watch various videos, keep an eye on the list of related videos to the right of the viewing box for others that might interest you. Take it all with a grain of salt.

Websites

The funny thing about some of these websites is that they look like they were built and put online in 1997 and haven't been touched since. In some instances, that might be the case, who knows. Most of these are just normal websites at least in design. By sharing these sites, I do not endorse ideas presented in part or entirety. This is simply for research. I must caution you that the background and persons behind these sites goes unresearched. Credibility is always a question when you ask questions.

- Journal of Debunking 911 Conspiracy Theories – I like to check out sites that debunk popular theories, so I can get a full view of all the evidence
- WhatReallyHappened.com
- Illuminati-News.com
- http://www.top-site-list.com/conspiracy – A massive list of conspiracy sites. You might also find this one useful to find sites for other interests
- http://www.jfkassassinationforum.com – A forum dedicated totally to the JFK Assassination

- http://www.wanttoknow.info
- http://www.pressfortruth.ca
- http://www.prisonplanet.com – Another Alex Jones site. Good info, high-paid informant
- http://letsrollforums.com/index.php – Forum mostly focused on 911
- http://www.debunking911.com – Research all sides
- http://vigilantcitizen.com – TONS of info and nice long articles with pictures
- http://www.disclose.tv – Video-heavy site with lots of information
- http://wearechange.org – We Are Change – I posted their corresponding YouTube channel above
- http://www.whale.to – This site is kind of strange. The domain speaks nothing of the contents. There's a lot of info on the site, but some of it seems a bit snake oil-ish, so be careful
- Russ Holmes Work File – Russ Holmes was a CIA archivist who maintained a large number of JFK documents. His work file was declassified in the 1990's
- http://vault.fbi.gov – FBI vault for declassified documents
- http://intheknow7.wordpress.com – The corresponding YouTube channel is in the list above. This one is a little crazy, but interesting nonetheless. The main focus is

Monarch Mind Control – an unconfirmed part of MK Ultra. So shocking, it's unbelievable

- http://truthisscary.com – Nicely done and interesting website
- http://www.aulis.com/index.html – Focuses on Space Exploration – has detailed analysis of Moon exploration photographs
- http://blindedbythelightt.blogspot.com – Be sure and check the vaccine resources on this informative site
- http://www.theblackvault.com – Nice website with TONS of info and detailed case studies
- Pilots for 911 Truth – The web home of an organization of professional aviators and pilots seeking the truth about 911.
- AboveTopSecret.com – The largest conspiracy forum on the 'net. It's well-moderated and a nicely designed site. This is the main site I visit for conspiracy stuff and alternative news. However, there is talk that it is a CIA front to find out what the public knows. I don't know a conspiracy site online that hasn't been accused of being a CIA front. All I can say, is BE CAREFUL.
- WorldNetDaily.com – Alternative news
- InformationLiberation.com – Another alternative new site taglined as "The News You're Not Supposed to Know"

- National Security Archive of George Washington University
- National Archives
- MarkDice.com – I included this site because I couldn't find anything negative about Mark's credibility that wasn't a forum post or from an equally hokey source. He writes a lot of exposes on major players in the conspiracy community.
- Coast to Coast AM – A long running AM radio show hosted by George Noory. They cover some CRAZY topics, but also host many interesting interviews.

This should get you started. As you research and read more, you will learn what topics you want to know more about and how to search for them. The above list are just ones I've handpicked for you from my bookmarks.

Some Favorite Threads from AboveTopSecret.com

- The Forgotten Victims of a Genuine Conspiracy – This thread comes from ATS user, RisingAgainst. He is well-known at ATS for his JFK threads that are well-research, image-packed, and just all around good reads
- Free 911 Researcher Starter Pack – A info-packed thread with a bonus link to the poster's UFO Research Starter Pack. ATS has some awesome content creators
- Power Downs Prior to 911 – 911 is such a complicated case because of the number of events leading up to the

day in addition to the events of the day itself. When you research deeper, you learn about these power downs, and other details like the drills the military was conducting that day. Real World or exercise?

- This Can't Be Happening in America – An overview of the insane things we've seen in America over the last decade
- Anagrams – A fun thread that plays around with an anagram generator and gets some crazy results
- Lee Bowers – A Murdered Witness – Another RisingAgainst JFK thread
- Mary Moorman – A Silent Witness – Another RisingAgainst JFK thread with new interviews with Mary after 50 years of silence
- Aliens and UFO's Are Really Demonic Spirits – This is not a popular idea, especially among the Atheist conspiracy crowd. Many theorists have written off religion as something that was created by man. I am not one of them; however, I think many conspiracies hold water without religion and politics playing a role in the evidence. I include this link to show you that there are people who think as I do, and there are people who oppose this belief as well
- The Smoking Gun – Another RisingAgainst JFK thread. These are just too good to pass up

- The Top 10 Conspiracy Facts of 2011 – A nicely written and well linked thread with a ton of info on theories that became fact in 2011

Books

I do most of my reading online. I've never been much of a reader. Don't get me wrong, I read books, I just don't devour books. You know what I mean? So, this list isn't as long as I would like it to be to appear educated and well-read, but what can I say?

I will be linking to Kindle editions when possible. No Kindle? No problem. Kindle apps for your iPhone, iPad, Android phone or tablet, computer, etc are FREE and you can find what you need HERE.

Or here: http://www.amazon.com/gp/feature.html?docId=1000493771

This will also allow you to find the books in other formats. Amazon usually has the best prices online for books. I'm trying to look out for you here. Without further ado:

- Who Really Killed Kennedy? 50 Years Later: Stunning New Revelations About the JFK Assassination – Jerome Corsi
- The Great Oil Conspiracy – Jerome Corsi – Other titles by Jerome (I keep typing James) Corsi may interest you as well: http://www.amazon.com/Jerome-R.-Corsi/e/B001HOHAGU/ref=ntt_athr_dp_pel_1

- JFK: The CIA, Vietnam, and the Plot to Assassinate John F. Kennedy – L. Fletcher Prouty **NOTE:** If you have ever seen the movie, JFK, and you remember the Mr. X. character from that movie played by Donald Sutherland, Fletcher Prouty is the man on which that character is based
- American Conspiracies: Lies, Lies and More Dirty Lies That the -- Government Tells Us – Jesse Ventura – Another profiteer in my opinion, but he covers interesting topics
- The Girl on the Stairs – Barry Ernest
- The Declaration of Independence, The Constitution, Bill of Rights, and Constitutional Amendments
- Holy Bible (KJV) – Kindle version with navigation
- Behold A Pale Horse – William Cooper – You can find this around the Internet as a PDF free download as well.

Software

- Google Earth
- FREE Bible from YouVersion – Android app that puts the KJV Bible on your phone or tablet FREE. Also download many other versions free

Suggested Search Topics

Are you hooked yet? Do you want to go deeper still? Here are some suggested topics you might want to investigate that are not covered in this book. Google or YouTube should give you HOURS of information.

- Global Economic Reset
- Bohemian Grove
- China vs. America
- Collapse of the Dollar
- Illuminati Symbolism
- Numerology
- Dulce Base
- Deep Underground Military Bases (D.U.M.B.'s)
- BP Oil Spill
- Bush/Bin Laden Connection
- Water Crisis
- Food Shortage
- Big Pharma
- Aurora Conspiracy
- Sandy Hook Hoax
- Boston Bombing False Flag
- Bob Lazar
- Area 51
- CIA and Drugs
- Federal Reserve
- War for Profit
- Prison Profiteers
- Majestic 12

- Project Bluebeam
- Technology Suppression – i.e. Hemp, alternative fuel, etc.
- Nikola Tesla
- Philadelphia Experiment
- Montauk Project
- HAARP – High Frequency Active Auroral Research Program
- TWA Flight 800
- NSA Spying
- A.I.D.S. is Man-made
- RFID Chips
- Tavistock
- John Lear
- Global Warming Hoax
- Big Foot
- Loch Ness Monster
- Jim Marrs
- Psyops
- Facebook and CIA
- Disinformation
- UFO's in the Bible
- Dinosaurs in the Bible
- Wikileaks
- Anonymous
- College Loan Conspiracy

- Declassified Documents
- Executive Orders
- Weather Modification
- UFO's   Caught on Tape
- Aliens   Caught on Tape
- Black Budget
- Black Contractors
- CIA Fronts
- 13 Bloodlines of the Illuminati
- Mag-Lev Trains
- Rand Corporation Tunneling
- Julian Assange
- Black Knight Satellite
- Michael C. Ruppert
- Occupy Wall Street

Appendix 1: Links in Order of Appearance

- http://youtu.be/kq1PbgeBoQ4
- http://youtu.be/pv_viK8qOfw
- http://youtu.be/Atbrn4k55IA
- http://youtu.be/qM98yIOOmzI
- http://youtu.be/KRTOB8JPwa8
- http://youtu.be/Wh4a3NVTJwA
- http://youtu.be/5rXPrfnU3G0
- http://www.cdc.gov/ncbddd/autism/topics.html
- http://news.nationalgeographic.com/news/2013/07/130716-autism-vaccines-mccarthy-view-medicine-science/
- http://www.naturalnews.com/041897_mmr_vaccines_autism_court_ruling.html
- http://www.naturalnews.com/038648_flu_pandemic_vaccines_shots.html
- http://youtu.be/RCdT69dhyvY
- http://www.geoengineering.ox.ac.uk/what-is-geoengineering/what-is-geoengineering/
- http://youtu.be/bSSWnXQsgOU
- http://www.wired.com/science/discoveries/magazine/17-05/ff_guidestones
- http://www.washingtonpost.com/politics/hillary-clinton-says-benghazi-attack-was-her-biggest-regret-as-

secretary-of-state/2014/01/27/bf842baa-8788-11e3-a5bd-844629433ba3_story.html
- http://www.amazon.com/Thanks-Memories-Memoirs-Kissingers-Mind-Controlled/dp/0966891627/ref=sr_1_1?s=books&ie=UTF8&qid=1391187067&sr=1-1&keywords=brice+taylor
- http://youtu.be/LrwiVkF8ig8
- http://youtu.be/Wu-SZY5bVr8
- http://www.youtube.com/user/ConspiracyStuff/videos
- http://www.youtube.com/user/intheknow7
- http://www.youtube.com/user/dutchsinse/videos
- http://www.youtube.com/user/Thepoliticalport/videos
- http://www.youtube.com/user/thepaulstalservice/videos
- http://www.youtube.com/user/AlltimeConspiracies/videos
- http://www.youtube.com/user/dark5tv/videos
- http://www.youtube.com/user/wearechange/videos
- http://www.youtube.com/user/DavidVonPeinJFK/videos
- http://www.youtube.com/user/TheAlexJonesChannel
- http://www.youtube.com/user/sbpitn/videos
- http://youtu.be/YsRm8M-qOjQ
- http://www.youtube.com/watch?v=Be0ow2Jjs9E&list=PL6D3AC36A1849B645&feature=share
- http://www.youtube.com/watch?v=KpBfbzxS1I4&list=PL6D3AC36A1849B645&feature=share&index=2
- http://youtu.be/-4scgRAJxWc

- http://www.youtube.com/watch?v=etgDxSUKLqc&feature=share&list=PL73A3930543D04773&index=21
- http://youtu.be/7LbNWUNfnaA
- http://youtu.be/bFhPEzQMSL0
- http://youtu.be/zKarTaDUxyU
- http://youtu.be/cMA8UvR9OjA
- http://youtu.be/iqpW89lhnE0
- http://youtu.be/hgMUmb-pWTo
- http://youtu.be/NGrrdTlMpS4
- http://youtu.be/-F-LY1HblmE
- http://youtu.be/2MQIIpJ2lmM
- http://youtu.be/BINQ4jiQFsI
- http://youtu.be/jf0khstYDLA
- http://youtu.be/C4h2czZTTLM
- http://youtu.be/pX-iP6JVqZY
- http://youtu.be/g4d2g9XIFnE
- http://youtu.be/Wpu6_kArb9U
- http://youtu.be/28kvrPXj-6U
- http://youtu.be/7DpPTdzpHGE
- http://youtu.be/oqHgG2KfLcU
- http://youtu.be/QJ22mk9SHIM
- http://youtu.be/pWA1Mc8aWhI
- http://youtu.be/L777RhL_Fz4
- http://youtu.be/aM1CkXxwf0Y
- http://youtu.be/_IR7HnCurkc
- http://youtu.be/byxeOG_pZ1o

- http://www.jod911.com/
- http://whatreallyhappened.com/
- http://www.illuminati-news.com/index.htm
- http://www.maryferrell.org/mffweb/archive/docset/getList.do?docSetId=1064
- http://pilotsfor911truth.org/
- http://abovetopsecret.com/
- http://www.wnd.com/
- http://www.informationliberation.com/
- http://www2.gwu.edu/~nsarchiv/
- http://markdice.com/
- http://www.coasttocoastam.com/
- http://www.abovetopsecret.com/forum/thread683402/pg1&addstar=1&on=10965957#pid10965957
- http://www.abovetopsecret.com/forum/thread420668/pg1&addstar=1&on=5494861#pid5494861
- http://www.abovetopsecret.com/forum/thread683023/pg1&addstar=1&on=10958855#pid10958855
- http://www.abovetopsecret.com/forum/thread694145/pg1&addstar=1&on=11168331#pid11168331
- http://www.abovetopsecret.com/forum/thread697040/pg1
- http://www.abovetopsecret.com/forum/thread710323/pg1&addstar=1&on=11471577#pid11471577
- http://www.abovetopsecret.com/forum/thread713461/pg1

- http://www.abovetopsecret.com/forum/thread716285/pg1&addstar=1&on=11586875#pid11586875
- http://www.abovetopsecret.com/forum/thread747232/pg1&flagit=747232
- http://www.abovetopsecret.com/forum/thread790231/pg1
- http://www.amazon.com/gp/feature.html?docId=1000493771
- http://www.amazon.com/Who-Really-Killed-Kennedy-Assassination-ebook/dp/B00EMFH0M0/ref=sr_1_1?s=digital-text&ie=UTF8&qid=1391184425&sr=1-1
- http://www.amazon.com/Great-Oil-Conspiracy-Government-Discovery-ebook/dp/B007VDECJ4/ref=sr_1_7?s=digital-text&ie=UTF8&qid=1391184425&sr=1-7
- http://www.amazon.com/JFK-Vietnam-Plot-Assassinate-Kennedy-ebook/dp/B004VX3D2Y/ref=sr_1_2?s=books&ie=UTF8&qid=1391184861&sr=1-2&keywords=fletcher+prouty
- http://www.amazon.com/American-Conspiracies-Dirty-Government-Tells-ebook/dp/B004N84I5S/ref=sr_1_5?ie=UTF8&qid=1391185184&sr=8-5&keywords=jesse+ventura

- http://www.amazon.com/Girl-Stairs-Barry-Ernest-ebook/dp/B00FAVZ9CS/ref=sr_1_1?ie=UTF8&qid=1391185568&sr=8-1&keywords=the+girl+on+the+stairs
- http://www.amazon.com/Declaration-Independence-Constitution-Constitutional-Amendments-ebook/dp/B0036Z9VFG/ref=sr_1_7?ie=UTF8&qid=1391185658&sr=8-7&keywords=declaration+of+independence
- http://www.amazon.com/Bible-James-Version-Search-Navigation-ebook/dp/B0055ECOUA/ref=sr_1_1?ie=UTF8&qid=1391185971&sr=8-1&keywords=holy+bible+kjv
- http://www.amazon.com/Behold-Pale-Horse-William-Cooper-ebook/dp/B007TOGYSC/ref=sr_1_1?s=books&ie=UTF8&qid=1391186159&sr=1-1&keywords=behold+a+pale+horse
- http://www.google.com/earth/
- http://www.amazon.com/YouVersion-Bible/dp/B004MC8CA2/ref=sr_1_4?ie=UTF8&qid=1391185971&sr=8-4&keywords=holy+bible+kjv
- http://constitutionus.com/
- http://www.wanttoknow.info/mind_control/cia_mind_control_documents_orig/
- http://www.wanttoknow.info/operationnorthwoods

- https://archive.org/details/SilentWeaponsForQuietWars_75
- http://www.maryferrell.org/wiki/index.php/JFK_Assassination_Documents
- https://archive.org/details/NewlyDeclassifiedCiaDocuments2012-Re9-11WarningsDeliberatelyIgnored-
- http://www2.gwu.edu/~nsarchiv/NSAEBB/NSAEBB381/
- http://ritualabuse.us/mindcontrol/mc-documents-links/

http://www.bibliotecapleyades.net/sociopolitica/esp_sociopol_mj12_3.htm

-

Appendix 2: Reference Materials

- The Constitution of the United States Online
- MKUltra Documents
- Operation Northwoods Documents
- Silent Weapons for Quiet Wars Document
- JFK Assassination Documents
- 911 Documents
- 911 Documents
- Project Paperclip Documents
- Majestic Documents

Afterword

Much of the subject matter presented in this book is just a starting point. Each and every subject goes so much deeper than the few paragraphs I've put together which are meant to just be a general overview of the topic. I cannot stress to you enough how important it is that you do your own research. It is also equally important that you ensure your research doesn't drive you mad.

If you've made it to this Afterword, your views have changed forever. Be vigilant. Be careful and cautious. Question everything. Stay strong in faith, hope, and love.

My Personal Views on Conspiracy Theories

NOTE: My views are even more unpopular than conspiracy theories. If you are an Atheist, you probably won't care what I have to say.

I'm Ava, and I'm simply a lone researcher who is trying to piece together the big picture from the bits of information I find around the Internet and in books. My main objective is to inform the interested public in my limited ways and knowledge of the injustices that surround us on all sides. I source my beliefs from the Bible and the Constitution and form my opinions from there.

The Beginning

The big picture begins when God gave Adam dominion over the Earth in Genesis 1:28. When Satan (Lucifer) tempted Eve in the Garden of Eden, and won her over with his promise of knowledge at which time she convinced Adam to partake as well, Satan assumed dominion over the Earth at that time. This is further illustrated in the Gospel of Luke when Satan offers all the kingdoms of the world to Jesus if he will turn stones to bread and eat to relieve his hunger (Luke 4:5-6). The Bible goes further by calling Satan "the prince of the power of the air" in Ephesian 2:2. The power of Satan resides within the atmosphere of the Earth.

Enter the Illuminati

I won't rehash information from the first portion of this book, but I believe the goal of the Illuminati was to put a dark plan into motion. I also believe the main influence on the Illuminati was Satan. So, since the early 1770's, that's almost 300 years, the big picture has been assembling under the influence of this organization controlled by Satan and his fallen angels. Some researchers claim that these fallen angels lay with humans to produce the Nephilim as described in Genesis 6. Noah and his family are said be the last remaining bloodline that was not corrupted in this manner. To be honest, this is just recent information for me and I haven't formed a solid opinion, but I have to say initially, it could fit in with my vision for the big picture.

The Elites, Secret Societies and Lucifer

Once we focus on more recent history, it's a bit easier to piece together what is happening. As a child, did you ever have a secret club? You and some friends might have built a clubhouse, and the main object of the club was to alienate others, whether they be boys, girls, or adults. Secret Societies are no different. I imagine that if you were asked, you could probably name 3 Secret Societies and 3 elites. In case you can't:

Secret Societies

- The Illuminati
- Freemasons

- Skull and Bones

Elites

- David Rockefeller
- Bill Gates
- Ted Turner

I believe that elites worldwide are involved in a Luciferian agenda. I think they take their marching orders from Satan, and that they do his bidding. I believe their rituals and practices are hidden in plain site and that they control pretty much everything.

Politics

I don't pretend to be an expert in politics because I'm pretty far from it. I do not believe in the two-party system. I simply believe that politics is a tactic to separate people and to create controversy so there can never be unity. I think elected officials and candidates are merely puppets who are paid off to do the bidding of a larger and darker "shadow government" of elite in the background.

My View on Conspiracies

As for my views on specific conspiracies, I'm not sure I've come to very many solid conclusions. I am somewhat non-committal in all areas except the ones presented as proven facts in Chapter 2. As I said early in this book, the truth is elusive. I describe my stance as such:

In researching conspiracy theories, I read the general idea, and sort of file it in the back of my mind. For example, several years back, I heard of these so-called FEMA camps. Around this same time, a random theorist came across a horde of plastic containers stacked in a rural area of Georgia. The theory was that these were coffins. This fed into a bigger theory that the BP oil spill was a plot to weaken the New Madrid fault and cause a massive earthquake. An earthquake in this region would devastate numerous Southern states and cut off supply lines to the West. Obviously, the result would be a large number of deaths, hence the stockpile of "coffins".

Further feeding into this idea was the failed result of the FEMA response after Hurricane Katrina. Also, there was a list of Executive Orders also publicized as a part of this entire theory that were merely waiting for the right disaster and martial law before they would be implemented. These Orders allowed for complete government control of things like transportation including seaports and airports, food resources and farms, electricity, and fuel. The Orders also allow for the registration of ALL persons in the U.S. and the ability to assign people to work brigades. It's crazy and scary to say the least. I did begin further researching these Executive Orders to find that some of them were from back as far as the Kennedy administration. Furthermore, many of them had been replaced with new Orders numerous times.

Things like this and all of these theories, I file into my brain under a sort of "just in case" idea that if "the s*** hits the fan", a popular phrase among conspiracy theorists, I will have a rough idea of what is happening. It sounds rather ridiculous when I write it down, but you must separate yourself from these truths when necessary so that you might have the abundant life Jesus promised. Just like I wouldn't spend all my time focused on a horror movie, or violent video game, I can't constantly focus on the gloom, doom, and terror that comes with these theories.

To put it simply, I have a solid distrust for government. Let me also say that I have an equal distrust for the conspiracy theorists who profit from this type of information. Some of the more well-known theorists make upwards of 6 figures a year touting this information along with survival food packs and other random things. Money is truly the root of all evil.

> *"When the last tree is cut, the last fish is caught, and the last river is polluted; when to breathe the air is sickening, you will realize, too late, that wealth is not in bank accounts and that you can't eat money."* - Alanis Obomsawin [48]

Whether you are a power elite pulling the puppet strings or a theorist selling your particular brand of propaganda, you are the same. The difference between theorists like William Cooper(his book was $25 in 1991; steep by today's prices) and say, whistleblowers, is that theorists profit and whistleblowers die. Again, listen, take note, file. Just like the truth is elusive so is corroborating evidence.

My truth isn't from any conspiracy website, although you might see similar thoughts in the conspiracy community, but my rough idea of the lay of the land is below.

The Historic vs. Scientific View

My views are often not often affected by the scientific view being a history buff. I lean heavily toward historical sources which may not always be solid. What can I say? I'm not sure the historical record goes unedited. I am equally unsure that the scientific record goes without editing as well. You can see how difficult this type of research is. To prove a deviation from common knowledge, especially a difference that is remotely shocking, is quite simply near impossible.

A Rough View of the Big Picture

Given the information provided in this book, and based on my beliefs above, I have pieced together a rough view of the big picture, and the proposed plan at hand.

In recent years, things are advancing toward an end at a feverish pace. I think that disclosure of a false alien agenda is at hand. I think aliens, which I perceive to be fallen angels or demons, will first be presented as friendly invaders offering us advanced technology possibly in exchange for resources. I believe this invasion will turn hostile, and it will seem feasible that the entire world unite under one government and one leader (the Antichrist) to fight our new alien adversaries. This will end ultimately in defeat at a great reduction in world population. At this point, the true colors of these aliens will become apparent, but at that time it will be too late. Satan will make his reign over the Earth known, and anyone who survives that is not of the elite caste will become slaves under this regime. Those who have sold out to Satan will live well during this time only to find in the end that they will burn for eternity.

Biblical Warnings of Things to Come

Whether you believe it or not, the Bible is a valuable historical writing. I personally believe that it is inerrant, God-inspired, and total truth.

> *"For we wrestle not against flesh and blood, but against principalities, against powers, against the rulers of darkness of this age, against spiritual hosts of wickedness in the heavenly places."* - Ephesians 6:12 NKJV

> *"Take heed that no one deceives you. For many will come in My name, saying 'I am the Christ.' and will deceive many. And you will hear of wars and rumors of*

wars. See that you are not troubled; for all these things must come to pass, but the end is not yet. For nation will rise against nation, and kingdom against kingdom. And there will be famines, pestilences, and earthquakes in various places. All these are the beginning of sorrows. Then they will deliver you up to tribulation and kill you, and you will be hated by all nations for My name's sake. And then many will be offended, will betray one another, and will hate one another. Then many false prophets will rise up and deceive many. And because lawlessness will abound, the love of many will grow cold." - Matthew 24: 4-12 NKJV

    Unfortunately, I don't see a deviation from this end. It may not happen exactly this way, but I believe that we are in the End Times foretold by Biblical prophecy. As I said, this is a very rough view, but I fully believe this is where we are headed as a people. There might have been an opportunity to prolong goodness 20 years ago, but I believe this time has passed.

    It doesn't get more gloom and doom than this, but there is hope in Christ. My faith is renewed each day by current events. I truly believe we are witnessing the times the Bible warned about. We are nearing the last generation of humanity. We have lived and died at the hands of people who staked a claim in Satan's plan for mankind just to experience wealth, privilege and control on Earth.

May *your* treasures be heavenly.

If you enjoyed this book, please check out these titles I've written under a pen name:

Did you know that American history is peppered with cases of human experimentation?

Could you in your wildest dreams imagine that it was happening through the mid-1970s? That is in most of our lifetimes!

I wish that I could tell you that it's a load of crap, but the fact is...it's true. Supported by dozens of declassified documents and publications, horrible human testing can be corroborated throughout our history. Conspiracy Fact: Human Experimentation in the United States introduces you to a number of appalling cases involving the most vulnerable members of society.

The book documents a handful of cases taking place between the 1840s and 1970s. That's right, for over a century, these atrocities were regularly happening. This is just the tip of the iceberg. Get it today.

Mind Control in the United States?

Hard to believe? The series Conspiracy Fact Declassified is back again to prove it happened. Through declassified documents and various other sources, we further explore human experimentation. This time we zoom in specifically on mind control and the Top Secret government projects that examined this realm.

We name the names.

This compelling book is sourced throughout. You'll find out about how the U.S. ferried Nazi scientists into the country after World War II, and how that single operation became the catalyst for the

creation of MULTIPLE experimental projects. You'll find out how those projects sourced more than 88 institutions nationwide to perform mind control experiments on unwitting citizens.
You will hear from survivors. Grab this one!

Visit my blog and sign up to my email list to be notified of future publications.

Bibliography

1. http://hnn.us/article/35445
2. http://www.jfk.org/content/pdf/reading-room/timeline/timeline.html
3. http://www.history.com/topics/9-11-timeline
4. http://news.bbc.co.uk/2/hi/uk_news/magazine/4443934.stm
5. http://rationalwiki.org/wiki/Moon_landing_hoax
6. http://www.dailymail.co.uk/sciencetech/article-2034594/NASA-moon-landing-hoax-New-photographs-silence-conspiracy-theory.html
7. http://www.history.com/topics/roswell
8. http://ireport.cnn.com/docs/DOC-426406
9. http://www.citizenhearing.org
10. http://publicintelligence.net/ssci-mkultra-1977/
11. http://www2.gwu.edu/~nsarchiv/news/20010430/index.html
12. http://constitution.findlaw.com/amendment4/amendment.html
13. http://www.noi.org/cointelpro/
14. http://investigations.nbcnews.com/_news/2014/01/06/22205443-after-43-years-activists-admit-theft-at-fbi-office-that-exposed-domestic-spying?lite

15. http://www.cdc.gov/tuskegee/timeline.htm
16. http://en.wikipedia.org/wiki/Human_experimentation_in_the_United_States
17. http://www.nature.com/news/human-experiments-first-do-harm-1.9980
18. http://www.bmj.com/content/315/7120/1437
19. http://www.bbc.co.uk/news/world-us-canada-11454789
20. http://www.sfgate.com/health/article/Serratia-has-dark-history-in-region-Army-test-2677623.php
21. http://www.cnn.com/2011/HEALTH/01/07/fluoride.recommendations/?hpt=T2
22. http://www.thefreedictionary.com/whistleblower
23. http://www.theguardian.com/world/2013/jul/30/bradley-manning-wikileaks-judge-verdict
24. http://www.theguardian.com/world/2013/jun/09/edward-snowden-nsa-whistleblower-surveillance
25. http://www.unc.edu/~ltolles/illuminati/Introduction.html
26. https://www.princeton.edu/~achaney/tmve/wiki100k/docs/Population_control.html
27. http://endoftheamericandream.com/archives/yes-they-really-do-want-to-reduce-the-population-22-shocking-population-control-quotes-from-the-global-elite-that-will-make-you-want-to-lose-your-lunch
28. http://www.un.org/esa/agenda21/natlinfo/countr/usa/natur.htm
29. http://en.wikipedia.org/wiki/Agenda_21

30. http://www.naturalnews.com/041897_mmr_vaccines_autism_court_ruling.html#
31. http://www.naturalnews.com/038648_flu_pandemic_vaccines_shots.html
32. http://science.howstuffworks.com/transport/flight/modern/what-are-chemtrails.htm
33. http://en.wikipedia.org/wiki/Eugenics
34. http://en.wikipedia.org/wiki/Eugenics_in_the_United_States
35. http://www.charlotteobserver.com/2011/09/26/2637820/wallace-kuralts-era-of-sterilization.html#.Uu_ebrSwXtQ
36. http://www.wired.com/science/discoveries/magazine/17-05/ff_guidestones?currentPage=all
37. http://www.globalresearch.ca/the-true-story-of-the-bilderberg-group-and-what-they-may-be-planning-now/13808
38. http://online.wsj.com/news/articles/SB10001424127887324244304578473533965297330?mg=reno64-wsj&url=http%3A%2F%2Fonline.wsj.com%2Farticle%2FSB10001424127887324244304578473533965297330.html
39. http://www.washingtonpost.com/politics/hillary-clinton-says-benghazi-attack-was-her-biggest-regret-as-secretary-of-state/2014/01/27/bf842baa-8788-11e3-a5bd-844629433ba3_story.html

40. http://www.vanityfair.com/politics/features/2008/05/monsanto200805
41. http://en.wikipedia.org/wiki/Ted_Gunderson
42. http://www.myfoxmemphis.com/story/18527976/former-memphis-fbi-chief-dies#axzz2sHtkeVbx
43. http://www.knowthelies.com/node/9095
44. http://ancienthistory.about.com/od/greekmedicine/f/HippocraticOath.htm
45. http://millercenter.org/president/speeches/detail/3677
46. http://www.merriam-webster.com/dictionary/euthanasia
47. http://www.markdice.com/index.php?option=com_content&view=article&id=114:william-qbillq-cooper-was-a-fraud&catid=66:articles-by-mark-dice&Itemid=89
48. http://quoteinvestigator.com/2011/10/20/last-tree-cut/

Printed in Great Britain
by Amazon